Pat, Cat, and Rat

TREASURE BAY

Parent's Introduction

Welcome to **We Read Phonics**! This series is designed to help you assist your child in reading. Each book includes a story, as well as some simple word games to play with your child. The games focus on the phonics skills and sight words your child will use in reading the story.

Here are some recommendations for using this book with your child:

1 Word Play

There are word games both before and after the story. Make these games fun and playful. If your child becomes bored or frustrated, play a different game or take a break.

Phonics is a method of sounding out words by blending together letter sounds. However, not all words can be "sounded out." **Sight words** are frequently used words that usually cannot be sounded out.

② Read the Story

After some word play, read the story aloud to your child—or read the story together, by reading aloud at the same time or by taking turns. As you and your child read, move your finger under the words.

Next, have your child read the entire story to you while you follow along with your finger under the words. If there is some difficulty with a word, either help your child to sound it out or wait about five seconds and then say the word.

③ Discuss and Read Again

After reading the story, talk about it with your child. Ask questions like, "What happened in the story?" and "What was the best part?" It will be helpful for your child to read this story to you several times. Another great way for your child to practice is by reading the book to a younger sibling, a pet, or even a stuffed animal!

> It was really funny when Tim hid in the can!

LEVEL 1 Level 1 focuses on simple words with short "a" and short "i" (as in *cat* and *sit*). This book focuses on the consonants b, c, d, f, h, m, n, p, r, s, and t.

Pat, Cat, and Rat

A We Read Phonics™ Book
Level 1

Text Copyright © 2010 by Treasure Bay, Inc.
Illustrations Copyright © 2010 by Meredith Johnson

Reading Consultants: Bruce Johnson, M.Ed., and Dorothy Taguchi, Ph.D.

We Read Phonics™ is a trademark of Treasure Bay, Inc.

Published by
Treasure Bay, Inc.
P.O. Box 119
Novato, CA 94948 USA

Printed in Singapore

Library of Congress Catalog Card Number: 2009929506

ISBN: 978-1-60115-312-8

We Read Phonics™

Visit us online at:
www.TreasureBayBooks.com

PR 11-14

We Read
PHONICS ™

Pat, Cat, and Rat

By Sindy McKay

Illustrated by Meredith Johnson

Say the Word

Help your child sound out some of the words from the story.

T...i...m. Tim!

Very good!

Materials: 5 simple items (for example, 5 pencils, 5 paper clips, or 5 pennies)

1. Find and point to the word *Tim* (page 6) in the book. Ask your child to say the separate sounds for each letter. Then, ask him to blend the sounds together to say the word. For example, for the word *Tim,* your child should say the sound for the letter "t," then the sound for short "i" (as in *sit*), then the sound for "m." Your child should then say the word *Tim.*

2. If your child says the word correctly, give him one item and move onto other simple words that can be sounded out.

3. If your child does not say the word correctly, say the sounds for "t," "i," and "m" yourself, and then blend the sounds together to say the word *Tim.*

4. Continue with additional simple three- or four-letter words from the story until your child has all five of the items. Possible words include *Pat, Dan, cat, rat, trap, bad, hid,* and *him.*

Memory

This is a fun way to practice recognizing some sight words used in the story.

1. Write each word listed on the right on two plain 3 x 5 inch cards, so you have two sets of cards. Using one set of cards, ask your child to repeat each word after you. Shuffle both decks of cards together, and place them face down on a flat surface.

2. The first player turns over one card and says the word, then turns over a second card and says the word. If the cards match, the player takes those cards and continues to play. If they don't match, both cards are turned over, and it's the next player's turn.

3. Keep the cards. You can make more cards with other **We Read Phonics** books and combine the cards for even bigger games!

where

he

see

my

put

be

there

good

down

I am Pat.

Dan is my cat.

Tim is my rat.

Dan can trap Tim.

Bad cat!

I am mad at Dan!

Where is Tim?

He ran fast!

He hid.

Where is he?

Where can Tim be?

Can Dan see him?

There is Tim!

Dan is in the can.

Good cat!

I pat Dan.

Dan pats Tim.

No, no, Dan!

Put Tim down!

Sit, Dan. Sit!

Good rat.

Good cat.

Rhyming

Can you think of another word that rhymes with can?

Pan!

Practicing rhyming words helps children learn how words are similar.

1. Explain to your child that these words rhyme because they have the same end sounds: *bat, cat, chat, flat, hat, mat, pat, sat,* and *that.*

2. Ask your child to say a word that rhymes with *Pat.*

3. If your child has trouble, offer some possible answers or repeat step 1. It's okay to accept nonsense words, for example, *lat.*

4. When your child is successful, repeat step 2 with these words:

   Tim   (possible answers: *dim, him, Jim, Kim, limb, rim, trim*)

   Dan   (possible answers: *ban, can, fan, man, pan, ran*)

   trap   (possible answers: *cap, flap, lap, map, nap, wrap, sap, tap*)

   bad   (possible answers: *dad, fad, glad, had, lad, mad*)

   hid   (possible answers: *bid, did, kid, lid, rid*)

   sit   (possible answers: *bit, fit, hit, lit, mitt, pit, wit*)

Guess the Word

This is a fun way to practice blending letter sounds together, which helps children learn to read new words.

1. Choose a simple word in the story that can be sounded out. Say the sound for each letter in the word. For example, for the word *Pat,* say the sounds for the letters "p," short "a" (as in *cat*), and "t," with a slight pause between the sounds.

2. Ask your child to guess or say the word.

3. If your child does not reply correctly, then repeat and extend the sounds. If your child continues to have difficulty, run the sounds closer and closer together.

4. Continue with additional words from the story, such as *Tim, Dan, cat, rap, trap, bad, mad, fast, hid,* and *sit.*

5. For variation, let your child provide the prompt sounds to you.

If you liked *Pat, Cat, and Rat,*
here is another **We Read Phonics** book you are sure to enjoy!

Big Cats

This nonfiction book offers a fascinating look at some of the biggest cats in the world. Lions, tigers, cheetahs, and even house cats—all in a book that is perfect for the very beginning reader!